Understanding
Islam™

Islam and Science, Medicine, and Technology

Sally Ganchy

ROSEN
PUBLISHING®
New York

For D & M, in honor of their curious expeditions

Published in 2009 by The Rosen Publishing Group, Inc.
29 East 21st Street, New York, NY 10010

Library of Congress Cataloging-in-Publication Data

Ganchy, Sally.
Islam and science, medicine, and technology / Sally Ganchy.—1st ed.
    p. cm.—(Understanding Islam)
Includes bibliographical references and index.
ISBN-13: 978-1-4358-5066-8 (library binding)
ISBN-13: 978-1-4358-5384-3 (pbk)
ISBN-13: 978-1-4358-5388-1 (6 pack)
1. Islam and science—History. 2. Islam and culture—History.
3. Technology—Social aspects—Islamic Empire. 4. Medical sciences—Social aspects—Islamic Empire. 5. Muslims—Social conditions.
6. Islamic Empire—Social conditions. I. Title.
BP190.5.S3G33 2008
297.2'65—dc22

                2008012611

Manufactured in the United States of America

On the cover: (*Upper left*) Egyptian professor Ahmed Zewail (*center*), winner of the 1999 Nobel Prize in Chemistry, receives an Honorary Doctorate at the American University of Beirut, in Lebanon. (*Lower right*) Takyuddin and other Muslim astronomers observe, study, and calculate the heavens at the Galata Tower observatory in Istanbul, Turkey, in this 1581 manuscript illustration.

CONTENTS

Introduction

In ancient Arabia, in the year 610 CE, a merchant named Muhammad had an experience that would change the course of history. According to Islamic belief, Muhammad was meditating in a cave on Mount Hira, just outside his home city of Mecca, when he heard a divine voice order him to "recite." Over the following years, Muhammad received many messages from the angel Gabriel, who conveyed God's exact words to the new prophet. Muhammad was illiterate, so he committed them all to memory. In time, he gathered a small group of followers, who learned his recitations by heart and kept them alive through oral tradition.

From these humble beginnings would be born a rich spiritual tradition, a major world religion, an enduring cultural flowering, and a mighty empire that would extend from the western edges of Europe

Worshippers bow in the direction of Mecca at a service in a Shiite mosque in Iran. Mosques include a small niche that points out the exact direction of Mecca, or the *qibla*.

to the easternmost reaches of Asia. Radiating outward from the Arabian Peninsula, the Islamic world would spread to Africa, India, Southeast Asia, Europe, China, and the steppes of Russia. At the height of the empire's strength and extent, a period known as the Golden Age, Muslim achievement in all areas of culture was unsurpassed worldwide. In the fields of science, medicine, and technology, in particular, the Islamic world shone brightly in an age often darkened by ignorance and incomprehension.

Some Golden Age scientific advances were made in pursuit of religious goals. For instance, anywhere they are in the world, devout Muslims must find the *qibla*, or the exact direction pointing toward Mecca, before kneeling to pray. The search for a reliable way to determine the *qibla* from anywhere within the empire inspired geographical and astronomical research. Islamic worship also demands good hygiene: Muslims must ritually clean themselves before praying. This focus on hygiene helped advance the quality of medical care in Muslim lands.

Last but not least, the Qur'an contains many statements in favor of scholarship. During the Golden Age, there was a widely held belief that science and Islam could not contradict each other. The better people understood the world, the more they would marvel at God's creation and the more devout and sincere worshippers they would be.

This book uses the term "Muslim science" to describe the achievements of Golden Age scholars. However, this term is not strictly accurate. Many innovators during this period were Christians, Jews, or even Zoroastrians. In Muslim lands at the time, people "of the book" (Jews and

Christians initially, though later the term included other religions) were allowed to practice their own religions and were not expected to convert to Islam. As subject populations, they paid a special tax, the *jizya,* which helped to finance the Muslim state. Although they did not enjoy complete social equality with Muslims, they did enjoy a level of freedom and opportunity that was uncommon for minority communities in most premodern societies. Their contributions are also part of the rich heritage of the Golden Age.

In the twelfth century, European scholars began translating thousands of works from Arabic into Latin, the shared language of European learning. These translators were particularly interested in rediscovering Greek and Latin works that had survived only in Arabic translation. They also translated original Arabic works on medicine, science, philosophy, and other subjects. These efforts helped stimulate the European Renaissance, a rediscovery of the ancient world that would revolutionize arts, science, and philosophy, and so transform the world.

The Rise and Spread of the Islamic Empire

Following his experience of divine revelation, Muhammad announced that the god who spoke to him, Allah, was the same god worshipped by Abraham, Moses, and Jesus. Allah had chosen Muhammad to become his last prophet and to deliver his final, perfect message to mankind. Muhammad proclaimed that all men worship and obey their creator. The name of the new religion, Islam, literally means "submission" to the will of God. The revelations received by Muhammad were eventually recorded in the Qur'an, Islam's holy book.

At first, the people of Mecca ridiculed the new prophet, and life for his followers in Mecca soon became very difficult. Many were persecuted and even killed. Thus, in 622 CE, Muhammad and a few of his followers moved to the nearby city of Yathrib, known today as Medina. This move marks the first year of the Islamic calendar. Muhammad became Medina's political leader. In time, he and his followers conquered Mecca. Muhammad rid Mecca's most holy temple, the

Kaaba, of its idols and returned it to its original monotheistic roots by declaring it the "House of God." Muslims believe the Kaaba was originally built by the prophet Abraham and his son, Ishmael, as a place for the worship of the One God. To this day, wherever they are in the world, Muslims pray with their bodies pointed toward Mecca five times a day. All able-bodied Muslims are required to make a pilgrimage, or hajj, to Mecca at least once in their lives, completing a physical and spiritual journey to the roots of their monotheistic beliefs.

A picture of the angel Gabriel appears in this late medieval manuscript. According to the Qur'an, Gabriel conveyed God's words to Muhammad and revealed wonders to him.

The Spread of Islam

Muhammad united the tribes of Arabia, and after his death in 632 CE, his followers chose a caliph, or successor to the Prophet. Caliphs were not prophets but political and spiritual leaders of the Muslim community. The first caliphs were chosen from Muhammad's original companions. Under their leadership, Muslim rule spread rapidly through Arabia, then Syria, Egypt, and present-day Iraq.

During what has been described as the first civil war among Muslims (656–661 CE), two groups fought over control of the caliphate. The first group supported Ali, the Prophet's son-in-law, who some thought should have become the first caliph. This group, known as the Shiites, believed that a member of Muhammad's family should lead the Muslim community. The other group, who were early advocates of what came to be the Sunni view, believed any Muslim could become the caliph. At the time, the governor of Syria, Mu'awiya, challenged Ali's leadership. Mu'awiya became caliph and passed the position on to his son, rather than some other Muslim leader, thus starting the Umayyad dynasty. Over time, theological and political differences between the Sunnis and Shiites grew. Shiites continued to support Muhammad's descendants as rightful leaders, whereas the Sunni majority of Muslims accepted the Umayyads and later dynasties.

The Umayyad Dynasty

The Umayyads extended Muslim rule through conquest, and over a long period of time, many people from those lands converted to the dominant religion. Soon, Muslims ruled Persia (modern-day Iran and Iraq), North Africa, the majority of Spain, present-day Afghanistan, Armenia, Azerbaijan, and parts of present-day Pakistan. However, the Umayyads favored Arabs (those peoples originating from the Arabian Peninsula) over more recent converts to Islam. Discontent grew among the new Muslims throughout the empire. In 750 CE, a group opposing the dynasty, led by the descendants of Muhammad's uncle Abbas and including Persian converts and Shiites, seized control of the empire. The new Abbasid dynasty (750–1258) ushered in a remarkable era of arts and learning: the Golden Age of Islam.

This Abbasid-era Qur'an was written in Kufic calligraphy, the oldest type of Arabic script. The Abbasids prided themselves on supporting scholarship.

The Birth of the Golden Age

In 762, the Abbasids moved their empire's capital from Damascus to Baghdad, a brand-new city in Persia. Thanks to the Abbasids' patronage of arts and science, the city became a flourishing cultural center. Caliph al-Ma'mun founded the Bayt al-Hikma, or the House of Wisdom, in 830. Part library, part translation center, and part research institute, the House of Wisdom attracted scholars from across the empire.

The Abbasid dynasty controlled lands that had once belonged to the successive empires of the ancient Persians,

Many of the Golden Age's most important translations and scientific works were written in the House of Wisdom, shown in this fourteenth-century painting.

Syrians, Babylonians, Egyptians, Greeks, Romans, and Byzantines. (The Byzantine Empire was the medieval-era, Greek-speaking Christian successor to the Roman Empire and was based in Constantinople, which today is known as Istanbul, in modern-day Turkey.) During the House of Wisdom's early years, scholars focused on collecting, systematizing, and learning from the knowledge of all these previous cultures. An especially important part of this process was the translation of books by Greek thinkers like Euclid, Aristotle, Plato, Archimedes, and Galen into Arabic. Translations made a vast new field of knowledge about mathematics, astronomy, medicine, and other subjects available to Golden Age scholars. Soon, new scientific works were being written throughout the new Islamic Empire.

Innovation

The translators, scholars, and scientists of the Golden Age were Muslims, Jews, Christians, and even Zoroastrian pagans. They hailed from North Africa, Spain, Persia, Central Asia, and Syria. But whatever their background, they were united by a common written language: Arabic. The unified Muslim Empire made travel and communication easy. Just as important, vital trade networks connected Spain and Africa with distant China. Ideas and innovations traveled these routes along with spices and silks.

Meanwhile, new technology helped to improve living conditions throughout Muslim lands. Agricultural innovations like better irrigation and new crops helped increase the size and wealth of the population. Literacy became common throughout the empire. The libraries of Córdoba and Baghdad both boasted more than forty thousand books. In contrast, most western European libraries during the same time could claim a few hundred books at most.

Eventually, the empire fractured politically as far-flung provinces slipped away from the Abbasids' grasp. However, this actually stimulated scientific and intellectual research, as various regional courts competed through arts and science.

SCIENCE

During the Golden Age, scholars across the Muslim lands made astonishing advances in astronomy, mathematics, physics, optics, chemistry, geography, natural sciences, and other fields. Their work laid the groundwork for the later European scientific revolution and Renaissance.

Muslim Astronomy

Muslims face the exact direction of Mecca, or the *qibla*, in order to pray. As the Muslim-ruled territories expanded, finding the *qibla* in places as remote as Spain and China posed a challenge. Without compasses, astronomers learned to locate the *qibla* by observing the sun and stars, then using spherical trigonometry to orient themselves toward Mecca.

Muslims pray five times a day: before dawn, at noon, in the afternoon, at sunset, and in the evening. Since prayer times are determined by the sun's position, they occur at different hours throughout the shifting seasons of the year. Precise astronomical observations and predictions were required to set exact prayer times.

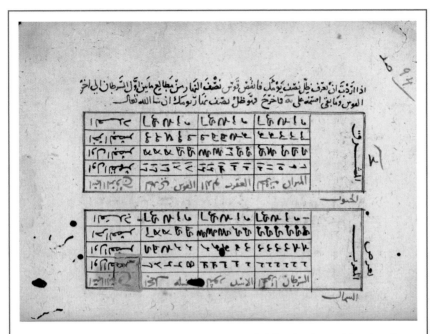

This table, from a ninth-century text by Ahmad al-Farghani, provides data for finding the exact direction of Mecca from a specific location using an astrolabe.

In the Islamic world, each new month starts when the new crescent moon is first sighted. This presents a problem: what if the sky is cloudy on the night the crescent moon appears? To accurately predict when the new moon would be sighted, astronomers studied the moon, its cycles, and its relationship to the horizon. Because lunar months are shorter than solar months, the months in the Islamic calendar shift through the seasons. Astronomers set dates for religious festivals, such as Ramadan, the holy month of fasting, based on the cycles of the moon. Many mosques employed a *muwaqqit*, or timekeeper, to set prayer times and festival dates.

Drawing on Ancient Astronomy

Hellenistic Egyptian astronomer Ptolemy's *Almagest*, or the *Great Book*, was translated into Arabic around 827 CE. This massive work collected the astronomical knowledge of the Greco-Roman world and remained the basis of Muslim astronomy for centuries.

The *Almagest* included instructions for using trigonometry to solve astronomical problems. It also provided tables of astronomical observations. Astronomers in the Islamic world added to Ptolemy's work with their own tables of astronomical observations, or *zijes*. These were made by teams of astronomers in observatories that were supported by generous rulers. Today, many important stars have Arabic names, such as Betelgeuse, Vega, and Aldebaran.

A Different Universe

The *Almagest* described the Greco-Roman model of the universe, which was very different from ours. Ptolemy's universe was geocentric: the earth stood still at the center of the universe, orbited by crystal circles that carried the planets, sun, and moon. Although this model of the universe was false, it explained many of the phenomena people could observe in the sky and accurately predicted many astronomical events. Ptolemy's model was actually very difficult to disprove without the help of a telescope, which would not be invented until approximately 1609.

European and Muslim astronomers alike generally accepted the geocentric model of the universe for centuries, seldom questioning the idea that the earth was the center of the universe. However, they did attempt to make Ptolemy's model of the universe simpler, more elegant, more accurate, and easier to understand. Over many years, the combined work of these Muslim critics posed a serious challenge to Ptolemy. The world was ripe for Polish astronomer Copernicus's heliocentric model of the universe—in which the earth orbits around the fixed sun—a theory first published in 1543.

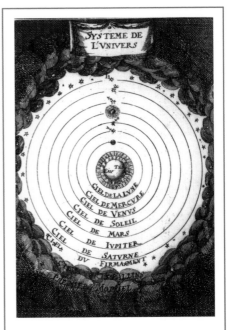

Some Muslim astronomers, such as al-Biruni and al-Sijzi, suggested a heliocentric (sun-centered system), but the geocentric model remained popular for centuries.

Mathematics

Muslim mathematicians set the stage for future greatness when they adopted the number system we use today: the Hindu-Arabic numerical system that originated in Indian mathematics. The new system was vastly superior to previous numbering systems, such as Roman and Abjad numerals.

Hindu-Arabic numbers made calculations much easier. Decimal points allowed mathematicians to use and calculate smaller and more precise numbers. The use of the symbol zero as a holding place opened up a whole new realm of mathematical possibilities. Hindu-Arabic numerals made it much easier to use numbers to describe anything from shapes to motions to patterns. This system reached the West through Arabic mathematical books translated into Latin during the early Renaissance. In fact, the English word "cipher," which once meant "zero," comes from the Arabic word for zero, *sifr*, which literally translates as "empty."

Golden Age astronomers pioneered new operations in geometry and spherical trigonometry, and mathematicians made advances in algebra and number theory. But perhaps most important, Muslim mathematicians combined previously separate branches of mathematics. By mixing and matching algebra, geometry, trigonometry, and arithmetic, Muslim scholars pointed the way toward the future.

Other Sciences

Western chemistry was born in Muslim civilization. The earliest Muslim chemists were alchemists, scholars trying to create an elixir that would turn any metal into gold. Through trial and error, they discovered processes like distillation and purification. Alchemical research led to the invention of antiseptics and modern recipes for soap and perfume. Our English word for chemistry has an Arabic root, as do the words "alchemy," "alcohol," "alkali," and "borax."

In physics, Ja'far Muhammad ibn Musa ibn Shakir, one of the famous Banu Musa brothers, contradicted Ptolemy's idea that heavenly bodies have their own special physics. Instead, he argued, all objects on heaven and earth obey the exact same laws of motion.

Persian scientist Abu Raihan al-Biruni made important advances in several fields. He was able to estimate the radius of the earth with a high degree of accuracy. A great traveler and geographer, he wrote about the habits, religions, cultures, and technologies of the people he encountered around the world. He is especially noted for his writings about and observations of India.

An alchemist is seen at work in this Arabic manuscript from 1399 CE.

Important Muslim Scientists

Many early scholars and researchers from the Golden Age were polymaths, or people accomplished in many fields. Mathematicians might study astronomy and physics. Zoologists wrote poetry and commentary on law. Doctors were also alchemists and astronomers.

Jabir ibn Hayyan (721–815)

Abu Musa Jabir ibn Hayyan (Latinized: Geber) was born in Iran in 721. He was a physician and apothecary, but his true passion was alchemy. In his quest to discover the philosopher's stone, which would be able to turn any metal into gold, Jabir tried thousands of different chemical reactions and became the first to describe many.

De A. Theuet, Liure II.   73
GEBER ALCHYMISTE ARABE.
Chap. 33.

In this European illustration, the alchemist Jabir ibn Hayyan, or Geber, is surrounded by chemical lab equipment that he helped popularize.

Jabir discovered many chemicals with practical applications. For instance, he learned how to chemically prevent rust and invented waterproof cloth. Jabir's texts were also the first to describe some basic equipment that is still used in today's chemistry labs.

His works were translated into Latin and became very popular among European alchemists. In fact, he and his works became so popular that later anonymous European alchemists wrote works under his name. Jabir's texts were written in highly symbolic codes designed to confuse those who did not already understand alchemy. For this reason, some people think that "gibberish," meaning nonsense, comes from the Latin translation of Jabir's name, Geber.

Al-Khwarizmi (c. 780–c. 850)

Little is known about the life of Muhammad ibn Musa al-Khwarizmi. He worked in the House of Wisdom, where he studied astronomy and geography. He is celebrated today for two books about mathematics. His *The Compendious Book on Calculation by Completion and Balancing* was the first significant book about algebra. In fact, the word

Alchemy and the Origins of Chemistry

The development of chemistry is intimately linked to the practice of alchemy: the search for a substance that would turn any metal into gold. Alchemists believed that everything that existed in the universe was made from four elements: earth, water, air, and fire. If they could change the balance of these four elements in a substance, they could change the substance itself. Alchemists sought a fifth element, the elixir, or philosopher's stone, which would be able to transform any metal into gold. Some alchemists also sought an elixir of life, which they believed could grant eternal life.

No alchemist ever found the philosopher's stone. However, the quest to discover it laid the groundwork for today's chemistry, which may be a far more valuable legacy than the sought-after elixir. Working with mercury, sulfur, arsenic, acids, gold, and other materials, alchemists in the Muslim world discovered how to create many important chemical reactions.

"algebra" comes from part of its title: *al-jabr,* or completion. However, by today's standards, al-Khwarizmi's early algebra was very clumsy and impractical. Algebraic symbols (like x and y) had not been invented yet, so he wrote out all his algebraic actions in words, rather than expressing them as mathematical equations.

Al-Khwarizmi's treatise *Al-Khwarizmi on the Indian Art of Reckoning* introduced Indian numerals to the Western world. We still use this system today, under the name of Hindu-Arabic numerals. The English word "algorithm," meaning a systematic approach to solving a mathematical problem, comes from the title of this book, which, in Latin, was called *Algoritmi de Numero Indorum*. The word "Algoritmi" is actually the Latin version of al-Khwarizmi's name.

Ibn al-Haytham (965–1040)

Abu Ali al-Hasan ibn al-Hasan ibn al-Haytham (Latinized: Alhazen), was born in Basra, Persia, but worked in Egypt. His most important work was as a pioneer of optics. He was the first to realize that light moves at different speeds through different materials, like air and water. He researched atmospheric refraction, magnification, and spherical and parabolic mirrors. He also made discoveries about how the optical phenomena of eclipses and sunsets work.

However, Ibn al-Haytham's most lasting legacy was not what discoveries he made but how he made them. The best example is how Ibn al-Haytham solved the mystery of how the human eye really works. Some ancient thinkers, such as Euclid and Ptolemy, believed that eyes shot laserlike rays of sight out into the world. Others, including Aristotle, believed that light entered the eye in rays. The two theories existed side by side for centuries. In his *Kitab al-Manazir,* or *Book of Optics*, Ibn al-Haytham broke the deadlock with a stunningly simple argument: if we look at the sun too long, we can still

VITELLONIS THV
RINGOPOLONI OPTI=
CAE LIBRI DECEM.

Inftaurati, figuris nouis illuftrati atque aucti: infinitisq́: erroribus,
quibus antea fcatebant, expurgati.
A'
FEDERICO RISNERO.

BASILEAE.

This illustration appears in a 1572 Latin translation of *Optics*, by Ibn al-Haytham. Today, Ibn al-Haytham is considered a pioneer of the scientific method. He set the stage for empirical science as we know it.

see the light when we shut our eyes. The light must enter the eye, not vice versa. Ibn al-Haytham went on to geometrically describe how rays of light enter the eye. He speculated that these rays are transformed into a picture by the brain. To test his theory, he created the first recorded camera obscura (see chapter 4 for a description of this device).

This simple argument represented a huge conceptual shift. Ancient thinkers believed that no phenomena, no matter how small, could be understood outside of a universal, overarching cosmic system. Any attempt to explain a phenomenon needed to explain the whole universe. Ibn al-Haytham's simple argument used real-world evidence to decide between two competing ideas. He did not care about conforming to a philosophical system. He simply experimented and analyzed the results. He thus set the stage for empirical science as we know it. In fact, Ibn al-Haytham developed an early version of the scientific method that included observation, a statement of the problem, hypothesis, testing, analysis, and publishing of results and conclusions. Earlier scientists had experimented, but this systematic approach to experimentation as the very core of scientific practice made Ibn al-Haytham a towering figure in the history of science.

Ibn al-Haytham's works were translated into Latin. They influenced important western European scientists, especially Roger Bacon, who would continue Ibn al-Haytham's work on optics. Through Bacon, Ibn al-Haytham's ideas would eventually lead to the development of realistic three-point perspective in Western painting. And Ibn al-Haytham's work on magnification and refraction would lead to the development of the telescope.

MEDICINE

The achievements of Golden Age physicians were partially built on Persia's rich medical traditions. The first Muslim hospitals may have been inspired by the famous pre-Islamic Academy of Jundishapur, which taught medicine, theology, philosophy, and science. Families of great Persian doctors dominated the practice of medicine in Baghdad during the early Abbasid caliphate.

Ancient Greek and Roman medical texts by authors such as Galen and Hippocrates were translated into Arabic in the early Abbasid period. These texts were prized by physicians. The scholars who translated from Greek often added their own observations to the texts. The resulting works could be more transformation than translation. For instance, Greek physician Dioscorides' book *De Materia Medica* described how to make hundreds of medicines from various animals, vegetables, and minerals. The Arabic translators of the book, however, added hundreds of additional medicinal materials, including many that Dioscorides may never have known about. The Greek original mentioned around six hundred plants; the earliest Arabic

This illustration from a 1224 Arabic translation of Dioscorides' *De Materia Medica* shows two doctors with a young apprentice. This book was translated in the House of Wisdom.

translations of the book mention roughly 1,500.

Many famous Golden Age physicians were non-Muslims who wrote in Arabic. According to reports, Salah al-Din (Saladin), the famous Muslim ruler who fought Richard the Lionheart during the Crusades, employed eighteen doctors: four of them were Christians, five were Jewish, eight were Muslims, and one was Samaritan.

Hospitals

Muslims saw it as a religious obligation to heal the sick, regardless of whether or not they could pay for medical care. Large cities in the Muslim world often boasted one or more hospitals that offered free care to all. Hospitals featured separate wards for eye diseases, skin diseases, surgeries, and other ailments. Some even had wings for the mentally ill. Areas for patient rest and recuperation were often attached to a garden with a fountain; the sound of running water and birds were thought to be therapeutic. Mobile pharmacies and clinics brought care to villages far from hospitals.

Universities

Medieval-era madrassas (literally "places where learning is done") established in the Muslim world in the ninth century were the world's first degree-granting universities. *The Guinness Book of World Records* lists Fez's University of Al Karaouine, founded in 859 CE, as the world's oldest degree-granting university. It is still operating today. Cairo's Al-Azhar University (founded in 975) offered classes in astronomy, philosophy, law, grammar, and logic. The two oldest universities in the European world were founded more than a hundred years later, in Bologna, Italy (1088), and Paris, France (before 1150). The Muslim world also boasted medical schools, many of which were connected to hospitals. These institutions granted degrees that qualified graduates to practice medicine.

There are many medieval Arabic medical texts denouncing or bewailing quack doctors and charlatans. However, in some areas, doctors and pharmacists were inspected and regulated by authorities. For example, in 931, Caliph Muqtadir asked his court physician to test all of Baghdad's physicians. The doctors were required to pass a test in anatomy and the works of Galen. If they failed, they would be banned from practicing medicine in the realm.

This illustration shows an Ottoman pharmacy, where two doctors describe how to make a prescription.

Muslim Medical Achievements

The Golden Age saw a huge number of medical discoveries and innovations. Muslim doctors were able to remove soft cataracts from eyes with a hollow needle. They learned about how antiseptics could be used to clean wounds, and they knew how to sew up wounds with silk or catgut. An important physician, Ibn Sina, described a kind of anesthetic whereby a sponge filled with sweet aromas and narcotics could be held over a patient's nose during surgery in order to ease his or her pain.

Muslim doctors were also fascinated by treatments for insanity and mental illnesses. Ibn Sina was intrigued by the connection between the mind and the body. In his works, we find the first descriptions of hallucination, dementia, paralysis, epilepsy, and insomnia, among many other disorders.

Another field in which Golden Age doctors made great strides was pharmacology. The Muslim world covered a vast realm, so physicians could acquire and use a wide array of plants, animals, and minerals in medications. The responsibility of the pharmacist, or the person who actually made medicines, was an extraordinarily serious and important one. In some areas, pharmacists had to pass regular inspections to make sure they were not cheating or poisoning their patients.

Important Muslim Doctors from the Golden Age

During the Golden Age, medicine was not as separate from other branches of science as it is today. It was not uncommon for astronomers and mathematicians to work as physicians also, and vice versa.

This European illustration shows al-Razi at work in his laboratory in Baghdad. He was the first to describe the distillation of petroleum and kerosene.

Al-Razi (865-925 CE)

Abu Bakr Muhammad ibn Zakariya al-Razi (Latinized: Rhazes) was born in the Iranian city of Rayy in 865. A man accomplished in many fields, including music, philosophy, and alchemy, he served as the court physician for the Iranian Samanid dynasty and was also the chief physician of hospitals in Rayy and Baghdad. Al-Razi is perhaps best known as the first medical author to describe smallpox. He explained what the disease is caused by, how to diagnose and treat it, and how to prevent it from spreading further.

A doctor's doctor, al-Razi was interested in the education of new physicians. His most important work was a medical encyclopedia, *The Comprehensive Book on Medicine*, which drew from Sanskrit, Arabic, Syrian, and Greek sources, as well as his own experience. It covered topics from skin and joint diseases to surgery to diet and hygiene. Al-Razi also wrote on subjects such as diabetes, kidney and bladder stones, and children's diseases. Several of his works were translated into Latin and became influential throughout Europe.

Ibn Sina (c. 980-1037)

Abu Ali al-Husain ibn Sina (Latinized: Avicenna) is often called the "father of modern medicine." He described his life in great detail in his autobiography, beginning with his precocious childhood in Persia. As a boy, he memorized the Qur'an by the age of ten, and by the age of eighteen, he was the personal physician to the local sultan.

Ibn Sina grew to be a man of exceptional abilities. His genius embraced many different disciplines: in addition to being an astronomer, alchemist, mathematician, and scientist, he was also a philosopher, poet, theologian, and statesman. Over the course of his life, he composed almost two hundred different treatises.

Ibn Sina made significant advances in pharmacology, physiology, and psychiatry. One of his greatest achievements was recognizing the contagious nature of tuberculosis, noting that some diseases spread through water and soil. He also published the very first known description of meningitis. Most important, Ibn Sina was the author of the influential encyclopedic medical textbook *The Canon of Medicine*, which the *Encyclopedia Britannica* calls "the most famous single book in the history of medicine in both East and West." Translated into Latin, the book became a touchstone for Western physicians. It was still being taught in the medical schools of Louvain and Montpellier in the seventeenth century.

Al-Zahrawi (936–1013)

Abu al-Qasim Khalaf ibn al-Abbas al-Zahrawi (Latinized: Abulcasis) was born in al-Zahra, a town just outside of the Spanish city of Córdoba. He became the court physician to Al-Hakam II, Caliph of Córdoba, a patron of learning. Al-Zahrawi's *Kitab al-Tasrif*, or *The Method*, a thirty-volume medical encyclopedia, covered surgery, medicine, orthopedics, ophthalmology, pharmacology, and more. Its celebrated chapter on surgery described hundreds of

The illustrations in a Latin translation of the famous medical encyclopedia *Kitab al-Tasrif,* by al-Zahrawi, provided guidance to Western doctors seeking to learn from the great Muslim physician.

surgical instruments, including many of his own designs. His work explained how to perform tracheotomies and tonsillectomies, as well as how to use surgical needles, scalpels, specula, the bone saw, and other instruments. Al-Zahrawi also wrote about how catgut, when used to sew up stitches, will eventually dissolve without a trace.

Ibn al-Nafis (1213-1288)

Ala al-Din Abu al-Hassan Ali ibn Abi-Hazm al-Qarshi al-Dimashqi was born in a town near Damascus and became the chief physician at Cairo's Al-Mansuri hospital. An early champion of dissection, he was the first to accurately describe many aspects of the human blood circulation system. For instance, he outlined how blood reaches the heart's right chamber and pulses through the pulmonary artery to the lungs, where it becomes mingled with air, then passes back to the pulmonary vein in order to reach the heart's left chamber. This description directly contradicted the earlier work of the Greco-Roman authority, Galen. It was just one of Ibn al-Nafis's many important physiological discoveries.

Al-Nafis had planned to write a three-hundred-volume medical encyclopedia. During his lifetime, however, he was only able to complete eighty volumes. Still, his incomplete work remains one of the largest medical encyclopedias in history and a towering achievement. Al-Nafis's work does not appear to have been translated into Latin until 1547, hundreds of years after his death. Shortly thereafter, European doctors made similar observations about blood circulation.

TECHNOLOGY

Since the Muslim-ruled lands stood at the crossroads of Europe, Asia, and Africa, exciting innovations spread throughout the civilized world quickly. Any new agricultural technique or type of astronomical equipment that caught on in Persia could travel easily to Spain. In fact, many of the technologies that defined the Muslim Golden Age did not necessarily have origins within Muslim civilization. The art of making paper originated in China, but it was the Muslims who spread the technology through the rest of the world. Other inventions had their roots firmly in the Arabic-speaking world.

The Incredible Astrolabe

Golden Age inventors created numerous astronomical instruments. Perhaps the most fascinating tool at a medieval Muslim astronomer's disposal was the astrolabe. Though the astrolabe was pioneered by the ancient Romans and Greeks, it reached its full potential in the Muslim world. An astrolabe consisted of many engraved plates, some specific to the user's latitude (his or her position in relation to the equator). An exact

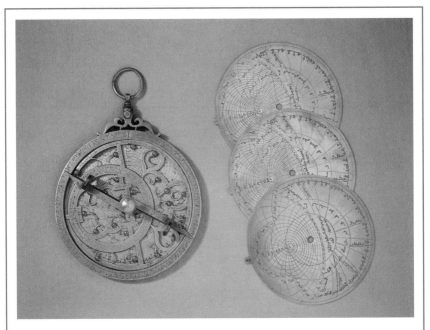

This beautiful astrolabe was created in 1216. Because it stored complex information in an easy-to-access form, the astrolabe is considered an early analog computer.

picture of the night sky, with positions of important stars, was marked on one disc. The astronomer started by taking the altitude of the sun or of a very bright star. When he turned the dials on the instrument to mark this altitude and the time of year, the astrolabe automatically showed the exact time of day, the *qibla*, and other useful information. Although the astrolabe was often used by religious authorities to determine prayer times and by scientists in geographic studies, some people used it to create astrological horoscopes. Arabic astrolabes served as models for later European versions inscribed with Latin characters.

Chemical Inventions

Given that the heart of the Muslim world is in the oil-rich Arabian Peninsula, it is hardly surprising that Muslim scientists first discovered or explicated many of the uses of petroleum. Al-Razi first described the manufacture and use of kerosene in his *Kitab al-Asrar*, or *Book of Secrets*. Kerosene was a safe, clean, and useful lighting fluid; in the 1860s, it became a common component of western European lamps.

Alchemical researches also produced new perfume recipes. Muslim scientists were first to describe how to use the new process of distillation to extract essential oils from flowers. They started with roses; hence, rosewater remains a popular fragrance today. The basic soap recipe that we use today was another by-product of Muslim protochemistry. "True soap" is made from lye, vegetables, and fragrant essential oils. Al-Razi was one of the first to write recipes for true soap. In 1200, the Moroccan city of Fez boasted twenty-seven soap manufacturers, many of which exported their soaps to European markets.

Amazing Machines

Ibn al-Haytham built the first recorded camera obscura, a device closely related to the pinhole camera. The device itself employs a completely dark room, or tent. A small hole, usually no bigger than a pin-prick, is created on one side of the room, facing a blank wall. Light from the outside enters the dark room through the pinprick, and when it hits the blank wall, it creates a complete and actual image of

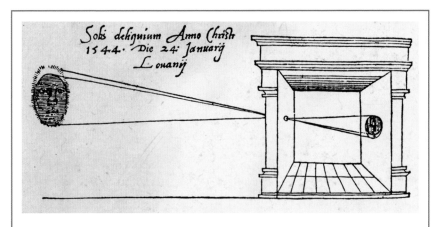

Solis deliquium Anno Christi
1544. Die 24: Januarÿ
Lovanÿ

Ibn al-Haytham was the first to describe how the camera obscura works. He used the device to safely observe a solar eclipse.

the scene outside. Ibn al-Haytham used this device to test his theories about light, including the ideas that light travels in straight lines. The camera obscura was one small step toward the invention of photography during the nineteenth century.

Muslim inventors also created colorful—though not entirely successful—flying machines. Inventor and scientist Abbas ibn Firnas attempted to fly in Córdoba, Spain, in 875 CE. He invented a kind of glider made out of silk and eagle feathers, and he leapt off a mountain with it. Historian Al-Makkari reported that eyewitnesses saw Ibn Firnas fly a fair distance. However, the sixty-five-year-old Ibn Firnas had forgotten to invent a good landing mechanism. He crashed but survived and lived another twelve years, to the ripe old age of seventy-seven. Today, an airport north of Baghdad is named after him. Much later, in 1638,

Ottoman-era scientist Hezarfen Ahmet Celebi built his own glider structure. He leapt from Istanbul's Galata Tower and reached the other side of the Bosphorus River.

The Art of War

The Chinese were the first to use saltpeter, or gunpowder. However, it was the Arabs who discovered a lethal gunpowder recipe by purifying gunpowder with potassium nitrate. Hasan al-Rammah described this purification process in his *Book of Military Horsemanship and Ingenious War Devices,* written circa 1270. His book contained 107 recipes for gunpowder and twenty-two sets of descriptions for building various rockets and other weapons.

Quilting might not sound like a military technology, but western Europe may have first discovered the technique in the heat of battle with Muslim warriors. Muslim armies wore quilted armor, which was lighter and more comfortable than Western knights' bulky, restrictive, and stifling armor. European knights who saw this armor while fighting in the Crusades brought it home with them. Quilts were soon being used as cold-weather bed clothing and as everyday clothing throughout Europe.

The Art of Living

Persia's most famous export product, carpets, is far older even than Islam. In 1949, a Persian carpet about 2,500 years old was discovered in Siberia's Altai Mountains. However, carpet-making technology was spread far and wide along with the advance of Islam throughout the world. After all, prayer carpets are an integral part of Islamic worship practices. During the twelfth or thirteenth century, most ordinary European floors were made of packed dirt or covered with rushes until carpets were introduced to Europe via trade with Muslim Spain.

Another invention that Muslims spread far and wide is today found in most American kitchens: coffee. Coffee was first discovered around 850 CE in Ethiopia, in a region named Kaffa. According to the old legend, an Arab goat herder named Khalid watched his goats eat the berry of the coffee plant and noticed that they became much more lively. Intrigued, he tried boiling the berries in water, thus creating

Prayer carpets are an integral part of Islamic worship and an essential part of Muslim culture. Here, a buyer looks at the Persian carpets for sale in the Grand Bazaar of Tehran, Iran.

Bringing Paper to the West

Papermaking originated in China around the year 105 CE. According to accounts, Muslims learned how to create paper after winning the Battle of Talas in 751 CE. This battle was the only time Muslim and Chinese forces fought each other. The Muslim forces took a few Chinese prisoners of war who knew how to make paper, and, soon after, paper was being manufactured in Baghdad. Paper was easier and cheaper to produce than parchment (flattened animal hides). Papermaking spread throughout the Muslim world, stimulating a new era of literacy. From the Muslim world, papermaking traveled to India and, by 1151, to Spain. It was through Spain that western Europe adopted the technology of papermaking.

the first coffee. However, it was through the Muslim Empire that coffee spread to other parts of the world. By the fifteenth century, coffee was being grown in southern Arabia, and the drink had reached Europe by the seventeenth century.

Earth, Water, and Wind

Muslim scientists wrote books on the subject of agriculture, and farmers developed and improved techniques such as the use of fertilizer. Crops traveled across the empire, taking root in new places. Lemon trees and sugarcane were just two of the crops introduced to many parts of the world, including Europe, through the Muslim Empire.

The earliest known designs for windmills came from Persia, between roughly 500 and 900 CE. These cylindrical windmills, which used between six to twelve sails made of leaves or fabric, were used to operate grain mills and water-raising machines, like pumps. The first illustration of a European windmill is dated 1270 CE.

Across the Muslim Empire, Muslim architects and engineers constructed reservoirs and aqueducts, some of which are still standing. In 1206, Al-Jazari became the first author to write about the crankshaft, a central part of modern machinery such as combustion engines. A crankshaft is a wheel that sets several crank pins into motion. The wheel's motion is circular, but the pins move back and forth in a straight line. al-Jazari's crankshaft was used to operate suction pumps, meant to help people pump hard-to-reach water with little effort. Al-Jazari also invented other water-raising devices.

The Banu Musa Brothers (c. 800–860)

Among the Muslim world's most famous inventors were three brothers. The Banu Musa brothers received the best possible education and went on to become scholars in Baghdad's House of Wisdom. They were among the first scholars to rediscover Greek works on mathematics. The brothers' most famous work is the *Book of Ingenious Devices,* an illustrated book that describes how to create about one hundred different machines. The Banu Musa brothers especially excelled in the creation of fantastic machines such as automata and trick fountains. One of their inventions was a trick pitcher. A host could pour three different colored liquids into the pitcher, one after the other, then pour them back out of the same vessel, unmixed and still displaying their original colors.

Al-Jazari (1136–1206)

Abu al-Iz ibn Isma'il ibn al-Razaz al-Jazari lived and worked in northern Mesopotamia. Little is known about him personally, except that he inherited his father's job: chief engineer for a local Muslim dynasty called the Artuqids. In his *Book of the Knowledge of Ingenious Mechanical Devices*, al-Jazari described many devices— some original and some older—that he had improved. Especially impressive were his automata. Al-Jazari created mechanical peacocks whose movements were powered by water, as well as a boat with four automatic musicians who played while floating on the water. Some historians think the robotic drummer could be programmed to play different rhythms!

Perhaps al-Jazari's most famous creation was his massive clock in the shape of an elephant carrying several figures on its back. Inside the elephant was a tank of water, containing a small bowl of water with a hole in its bottom. The bowl took exactly a half hour to fill and sink. The sinking bowl tugged a rope connected to a figure of a scribe riding on the elephant's back. This scribe turned in a slow semicircle, a little farther with each minute, acting much like a clock's

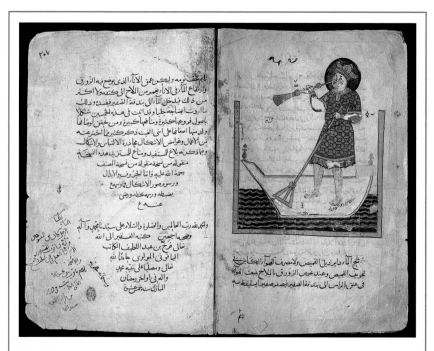

This illustration is from an Egyptian manuscript of al-Jazari's *Book of the Knowledge of Ingenious Mechanical Devices*. The boat in this picture has a small hole in the bottom and takes precisely one hour to sink.

minute hand. When the bowl finally sank, it pulled a rope that released a singe metal ball in the clock's cupola. The ball fell into the mouth of a serpent, weighting the serpent's mouth down. As the serpent's head fell, his tail rose, pulling up the rope connected to the half-hour bowl, and so resetting the clock. Meanwhile, another automaton was set in motion: an elephant driver who struck the hour on a drum. A disc on the top of the clock showed how many hours had passed since sunrise (or sunset).

BEYOND THE GOLDEN AGE

In the eleventh century, the Abbasid Empire began to crumble. The Abbasid caliphs continued to lead the Muslim world, but in name only. Political power was seized by local dynasties, like the Seljuk dynasty in Persia and the Fatimid dynasty in Egypt.

The End of the Golden Age

The Muslim world was weakened further by outside attack. From 1095 to 1291 CE, Christian Europeans, urged by the Catholic Church, launched a series of Crusades, or holy wars, against the Muslim world. The Crusaders were bent on conquering sites holy to Christians in the Middle East. Although the Crusades were ultimately unsuccessful, they created some disruption in the Muslim world and, ironically, spread many Muslim technologies to Europe.

Meanwhile, Spain was slowly slipping out of Muslim hands. For centuries, the political lines between Muslim and Christian were constantly being redrawn. From the mid-eleventh century CE onward, Christian rulers began serious attempts to conquer the Muslim-ruled territories in the southern part of the Iberian Peninsula. In European sources, this long conflict is called the Reconquista, or Reconquest.

Over the centuries, Muslim scholars attempted to interpret the teachings of Islam in light of the political, economic, and social conditions they faced. Scholars debated the relative importance of reason and divine revelation in managing individual and collective life. They also held various opinions on the relationship between strict adherence to religious law, inner spiritual development (including mysticism), and philosophical exploration. Influential theologian al-Ghazali (1058–1111 CE) argued that reason alone was not a sufficient or fulfilling path to achieving faith. Al-Ghazali is noted for harmonizing these various strands in a way that was acceptable to many Muslims in the following centuries.

Christian forces conquered Granada, the last remaining Muslim kingdom in Spain in 1492. The same year, Spanish King Ferdinand and Queen Isabella sent Christopher Columbus west to find the Indies, a voyage of exploration during which he accidentally discovered the Americas. They also set out to make their kingdom the most Christian in Europe. They forced all Jews to convert to Catholicism and exiled those Jews who refused. In 1502, Spanish Muslims were also ordered to convert. The Spanish Inquisition, a special religious court, was charged with discovering secret Jews, Muslims, and Christians that the Church considered heretics.

In the thirteenth century, the Abbasid capital was destroyed by the Mongols. Mongol armies had already swept across Asia, conquering lands from the Pacific Ocean

This fourteenth-century historical manuscript shows the Mongols, led by Hulegu Khan, storming Baghdad in 1258. Among the treasures lost in the invasion was the House of Wisdom.

to the Black Sea to the Indian and Arabian Oceans. In 1258, the armies of Hulegu Khan (grandson of the fearsome Genghis Khan) destroyed Baghdad. The Mongols tore down the walls of the city and slaughtered thousands of Muslims—reports range from two hundred thousand to more than a million killed. Among those slaughtered was the last Abbasid caliph. Baghdad's great libraries were destroyed. Thousands of books were burned or thrown into the river. According to one story, the Tigris River was packed so tightly with books that a horse could walk across its top.

The Muslim world was now a collection of competing dynasties without even a nominal center. Although the following centuries would bring some scientific advances, the Golden Age was over.

Islamic History Beyond the Golden Age

By the year 1500, the Muslim world included the Songhai Empire in Western Africa, the Sultanate of Delhi in India,

A Shared Legacy

Today, Islam's impact on our own heritage can be seen in words we inherit from Arabic, many of them used in discussing science and astronomy, or technologies that reached the West through Muslim lands. These words include alchemy, alcohol, alfalfa, algebra, algorithm, alkali, aorta, artichoke, apricot, diaphragm, cipher, caliber, coffee, colon, cotton, elixir, nadir, pancreas, sofa, syrup, tariff, and zenith. Many names of important stars, including Aldebaran and Betelgeuse, also come from Arabic.

and Pakistan. Much of the eastern coast of Africa and Madagascar also became Muslim, as did parts of South East Asia.

Muslim Empires grew, flourished, and fell in Persia and India. In the early fourteenth century, the Ottoman Empire, headed by powerful warrior Turks, took over Asia Minor. Under the sultan Suleyman the Magnificent (1494–1566), the empire stretched from the European Balkan Mountains to Egypt and North Africa. However, after Suleyman's death, the Ottoman Empire's power was increasingly challenged by newly assertive European countries.

The Europeans conquered the high seas, and trade routes shifted away from Muslim Arabia and Asia Minor. As European powers grew more wealthy and powerful, they began conquering colonies in Muslim lands such as India and Pakistan, Syria, Lebanon, and Algeria. After World War I, the European victors dissolved the Ottoman Empire, making its Middle East provinces into protectorates, and the Ottoman heartland in Anatolia became the modern state of Turkey.

In the twentieth century, independence movements gradually freed one land after another from European domination. Today's Muslim world is a rich tapestry, featuring many different cultures and forms of government, from the modern secular republic of Turkey to the theocratic state in Iran.

Muslim Scientists in the Twentieth Century

The twentieth and twenty-first centuries have benefited from the work of great scientists of Muslim origin, many of them living and working in North America.

Muslim Astronauts

Many Muslims participated in the space race—the competition to see whether the United States or its rival the Soviet Union (USSR) would be the first to put a man on the moon.

Egyptian-born scientist Farouk El-Baz worked for the United States' space program, the National Aeronautics and Space Administration (NASA), from 1967 to 1972. He helped to select the site for the U.S. moon landing in 1969 and was chairman of the Astronaut Training Group. In fact, when astronaut Alfred Worden orbited the moon in the

Apollo 15 spacecraft, he told his ground crew, "After the King [El-Baz]'s training, I feel like I've been here before." El-Baz went on to lead a center at the Smithsonian's National Air and Space Museum in Washington.

In 1985, Saudi Arabian prince Sultan bin Salman bin Abdulaziz Al Saud became the first Muslim to reach space. In 2006, Iranian-born American Anousheh Ansari became the first Muslim woman in space, making a visit to the International Space Station. And in 2007, Malaysian astronaut Dr. Sheikh Muszaphar Shukor became the first doctor to conduct medical research in space.

Nobel Prize–winning chemist Ahmed Zewail, on the right, meets with Sheikh Mohammed bin Rashid Al Maktoum, crown prince of Dubai.

Chemistry

Ahmed Zewail was born in 1946 in Damanhur, Egypt. Growing up, he was fascinated by the physics of chemistry. He earned his undergraduate and master's degrees in Egypt, and his Ph. D. studies took him to the United States, where he became a respected and sought-after scientist.

Zewail won the 1999 Nobel Prize for the development of femtochemistry, the study of chemical reactions that take place in less than the blink of an eye. Zewail developed a technique of photographing chemical reactions using a laser flash, capturing images of the reaction in femtosecond increments. How small is a femtosecond? Consider this statement by the Nobel Prize committee: a femtosecond "is to a second as a second is to thirty-two million years." Femtochemistry has enabled scientists to understand exactly why and how the most basic chemical reactions really happen, moment by moment. Zewail made it possible for scientists worldwide to understand chemistry in a way never before possible.

Chicago's famous Sears Tower, engineered by Fazlur Rahman Khan, was the United States' tallest building as of 2008.

Engineering

Fazlur Rahman Khan (1929–1982) was one of America's most famous civil engineers. He was born in Dakha, in the Bengal region of India, but it was in Chicago, Illinois, that he truly made his mark. He lived and worked at a time when the United States' population was rapidly expanding. Finding enough space for housing and offices in big cities was becoming a major challenge. Skyscrapers seemed to be one solution, but they were too expensive to build. The taller the building, the stronger and stiffer it needed to be to resist the wind, but steel was a costly building material.

Khan found several brilliant solutions to this problem. He pioneered the bundled tube structural system, which replaced old solid-steel beams with groups of thin-but-strong steel cylinders that, joined together, became very strong columns. This and other Khan innovations made skyscrapers stronger, more efficient, and less expensive. He engineered Chicago's John Hancock Center (1970) and Sears Tower (1973), which was the tallest building in the world for many years.

Khan also designed a special airport terminal for the King Abdulaziz International Airport in Saudi Arabia. Khan's Hajj Terminal is used only during the annual Muslim pilgrimage. More than two million pilgrims on their way to Mecca and Medina use the airport each hajj season. The world's fourth-largest air terminal, it is meant to shelter up to eighty thousand pilgrims at a time. It has no walls. The roof, made out of fiberglass, appears to be a long series of tents, sheltering travelers from the desert sun.

Pierre Omidyar, founder of eBay, is a billionaire who believes in using his wealth to help others. His Omidyar Network helps people achieve their dreams through grants and investments.

Computer Science

Although he was born in France, Iranian-American Pierre Omidyar is one of America's most successful businessmen. He is the man who founded eBay, currently the world's most successful online auction site. Connecting millions of people across the globe, eBay allows them to easily buy, sell, and trade practically anything—from collectibles and cars to appliances and books. The company had approximately 276 million registered users as of 2007. Today, Omidyar is a billionaire and philanthropist.

Jawed Karim was born in Merseberg, East Germany, in 1979 to a Bangladeshi father and an American mother. As a college student studying computer science in Illinois, he took a job at the e-payment site called PayPal. There, he met Chad Hurley and Steve Chen, who would become his friends and partners. Karim said that he came up with the idea for YouTube when he had difficulty finding online videos of the massive tsunami that devastated coastal South Asia. His partners thought a video-hosting service would be a good idea, and YouTube was born.

Karim helped get YouTube off the ground with technical support and ideas. Soon after he provided this consulting and advice, he began attending Stanford University for graduate school in computer science. YouTube went on to become a global phenomenon, the world's favorite destination to share, watch, and comment on videos. It has revolutionized the way that people think about, view, and make videos. Karim remained an adviser to the company, and when YouTube was bought by the Internet search engine company Google in 2006, he became a multimillionaire.

The Future of Muslim Science, Medicine, and Technology

Each generation of scientists builds on the discoveries of the past. From the Golden Age of Islam to the present day, Muslim scientists have been a part of the global triumph of science. In the twenty-first century, Muslim scientists will continue to work with scientists from around the world on the challenges and opportunities that face humanity.

GLOSSARY

altitude The elevation of a certain object above the horizon. Astronomers look for the altitude of celestial objects in the sky.

anesthetic A drug meant to numb the body or put a patient to sleep. Anesthetic is often used during surgery or other painful procedures.

astronomy The study of celestial objects.

caliph Literally, "a successor to Muhammad." Caliph was originally the title of the spiritual, political, and military leader of the entire Muslim community. However, as time progressed and different figures ruled the various Muslim lands, the title became more symbolic.

cataract A cloudy area on the eye capable of blurring one's vision.

dynasty A line of rulers descended from one family.

heliocentric Literally, "centered around the sun." Heliocentric often refers to the current idea of how the solar system is configured, with planets revolving around the sun. It is the opposite of the geocentric (or Earth-centered) model of the universe, in which the planets and stars revolve around Earth.

mosque A Muslim place of worship.

observatory A place where astronomical observations are made, often with large or expensive astronomical equipment.

optics The science of light and vision. It deals with how light behaves and how visual phenomena are created.

petroleum Another name for crude oil. It can also be used to describe oil products in general.

pharmacist A person trained to make and dispense medicines.

Qur'an Islam's holy book (sometimes written in English as "Koran"). Muslims believe the Qur'an is the word of God as revealed to Muhammad.

Renaissance The Renaissance, or "rebirth," was an era (roughly 1450–1600 CE) when western Europe rediscovered ancient Greek and Roman philosophy, art, and culture. One of the significant cultural developments to emerge from the Renaissance was the Western world's interest in science and mathematics.

trigonometry A branch of mathematics that deals with right triangles. Trigonometry may be used in practical applications such as engineering and navigation.

tuberculosis A dangerous, infectious, airborne disease that affects the lungs.

FOR MORE INFORMATION

Chemical Heritage Foundation
315 Chestnut Street
Philadelphia, PA 19106
(215) 925-2222
Web site: http://www.chemheritage.org
The Chemical Heritage Foundation is dedicated to educating the public about the chemical and molecular sciences, technologies, and industries.

Foundation for Science, Technology, and Civilization
10 Carlton House Terrace
London, England SW1Y 5AH
Tel.: 44 207 321 2220
Web site: http://www.muslimheritage.com
The goal of this educational foundation, which is based in the United Kingdom, is to inform the public about Muslim contributions to science and technology.

History of Science Society
P.O. Box 117360
3310 Turlington Hall
University of Florida
Gainesville, FL 32611-7360
(352) 392-1677
Web site: http://www.hssonline.org

This worldwide organization is dedicated to studying medicine, science, and technology. The History of Science Society also focuses on the historical relationship of these disciplines with society.

Institute on Religion and Civic Values (IRCV)
10055 Slater Avenue, Suite 250
Fountain Valley, CA 92708
(714) 839-2929
Web site: http://www.ircv.org
IRCV is a national, nonprofit research center with expertise in world history, world religions, and inter-religious and civic issues. Its Web site includes lesson plans and resources on these topics for educators.

U.S. National Library of Medicine
History of Medicine Division
Building 38, Room 1E-21
8600 Rockville Pike
Bethesda, MD 20894
Web site: http://www.nlm.nih.gov/hmd/index.html
The National Library of Medicine is home to an impressive collection of books and other materials about medicine and health throughout history.

Web Sites

Due to the changing nature of Internet links, Rosen Publishing has developed an online list of Web sites related to the subject of this book. This site is updated regularly. Please use this link to access the list:

http://www.rosenlinks.com/ui/ismt

FOR FURTHER READING

Corzine, Phyllis. *World History Series—The Islamic Empire*. Chicago, IL: Lucent Books, 2004.

Doak, Robin. *Empire of the Islamic World*. New York, NY: Facts on File, 2004.

Lombard, Maurice. *The Golden Age of Islam*. Princeton, NJ: Markus Wiener Publishers, 2003.

Lowney, Chris. *A Vanished World: Medieval Spain's Golden Age of Enlightenment*. New York, NY: Free Press, 2005.

Meri, Josef W., ed. *Medieval Islamic Civilization: An Encyclopedia*. New York, NY: Taylor & Francis Group, 2006.

Morgan, Michael Hamilton. *Lost History: The Enduring Legacy of Muslim Scientists, Thinkers, and Artists*. Washington, DC: National Geographic, 2007.

Morris, Neil. *The Atlas of Islam: People, Daily Life, and Traditions*. Hauppauge, NY: Barron's Educational Series, 2003.

Spilsbury, Richard, and Louise Spilsbury. *The Islamic Empires* (Time Travel Guides). Chicago, IL: Raintree, 2008.

Wallace-Murphy, Tim. *What Islam Did for Us: Understanding Islam's Contribution to Western Civilization*. London, England: Watkins, 2006.

Yount, Lisa. *The History of Medicine* (World History Series). Chicago, IL: Lucent Books, 2001.

BIBLIOGRAPHY

Armstrong, Karen. *Islam: A Short History*. New York, NY: The Modern Library, 2000.

Covington, Richard. "Rediscovering Arabic Science." *Saudi Aramco World*, May/June 2007, Vol. 58, No. 3. Retrieved February 2008 (http://www.saudiaramcoworld. com/issue/200703/rediscovering.arabic.science.htm).

Frazier, Ian. "Invaders: Destroying Baghdad." *New Yorker*, April 25, 2005. Retrieved February 2008 (http://www. newyorker.com/archive/2005/04/25/050425fa_fact4).

FSTC Limited. "Machines of Al-Jazari and Taqi Al-Din." December 30, 2004. Retrieved February 2008 (http:// www.muslimheritage.com/topics/default.cfm?Taxonomy TypeID=103&TaxonomySubTypeID=24&Taxonomy ThirdLevelID=-1&ArticleID=466).

George, Linda S. *The Golden Age of Islam*. New York, NY: Benchmark Books, 1998.

Gingerich, Owen. "Islamic Astronomy." *Scientific American*, April 1986. Retrieved February 2008 (http://www. faculty.kfupm.edu.sa/PHYS/alshukri/PHYS215/ Islamic%20astronomy.htm).

Haskins, Charles H. "Arabic Science in Western Europe." *Isis*, Vol. 7, No. 3, 1925, pp. 478–485.

al-Hassan, Ahmad Y. "Al-Jazari and the History of the Water Clock." History of Science and Technology in

Islam. Retrieved February 2008 (http://www.history-science-technology.com/Articles/articles%206.htm).

al-Hassan, Ahmad Y. "Gunpowder Composition for Rockets and Cannon in Arabic Military Treatises in Thirteenth and Fourteenth Centuries." History of Science and Technology in Islam. Retrieved February 2008 (http://www.history-science-technology.com/Articles/articles%202.htm).

Hoberman, Barry. "The Battle of Talas." *Saudi Aramco World*, September/October 1982. Retrieved February 2008 (http://www.saudiaramcoworld.com/issue/198205/the.battle.of.talas.htm).

Irwin, Robert. "Islamic Science and the Long Siesta." Times (UK) Online. January 23, 2007. Retrieved February 2008 (http://entertainment.timesonline.co.uk/tol/arts_and_entertainment/the_tls/article3237245.ece).

Lienhard, John. "No. 1910: 'Abbas Ibn Firnas.'" Engines of Our Ingenuity. Retrieved February 2008 (http://www.uh.edu/engines/epi1910.htm).

Lindberg, David. *The Beginnings of Western Science*. Chicago, IL: University of Chicago Press, 1992.

National Library of Medicine. "Islam and the Medical Arts: Medieval Islamic Medicine." Retrieved February 2008 (http://www.nlm.nih.gov/exhibition/islamic_medical/islamic_02.html).

O'Connor, J. J., and E. F. Robertson. "Al-Haytham." MacTutor History of Mathematics, November 1999. Retrieved February 2008 (http://www.history.mcs.st-andrews.ac.uk/Biographies/Al-Haytham.html).

O'Connor, J. J., and E. F. Robertson. "Arabic Mathematics: Forgotten Brilliance?" MacTutor History of Mathematics, November 1999. Retrieved February 2008 (http://www.history.mcs.st-andrews.ac.uk/HistTopics/Arabic_mathematics.html).

O'Connor, J. J., and E. F. Robertson. "Banu Musa." MacTutor History of Mathematics, November 1999. Retrieved February 2008 (http://www.history.mcs.st-andrews.ac.uk/Biographies/Banu_Musa.html).

O'Connor, J. J., and E. F. Robertson. "Muhammad ibn Musa Al-Khwarizmi." MacTutor History of Mathematics. November 1999. Retrieved February 2008 (http://www.history.mcs.st-andrews.ac.uk/Biographies/Al-Khwarizmi.html).

Overbye, Dennis. "How Islam Won, and Lost, the Lead in Science." *New York Times*, October 30, 2001. Retrieved February 2008 (http://www.google.com/search?client=safari&rls=en&q=new+york+times+how+islam+won,+and+lost,+the+lead+in+science&ie=UTF-8&oe=UTF-8).

Turner, Howard. *Science in Medieval Islam.* Austin, TX: University of Texas Press, 1997.

University of Cambridge. "An Islamic Astrolabe." Retrieved February 2008 (http://www.hps.cam.ac.uk/starry/isaslabe.html).

Whitaker, Brian. "Centuries in the House of Wisdom." Guardian (UK) Online, September 23, 2004. Retrieved February 2008 (http://education.guardian.co.uk/higher/research/story/0,,1310306,00.html).

INDEX

About the Author

Sally Ganchy is a writer and educator currently living in Budapest, Hungary. She is fascinated by the history of science and has traveled through Egypt, Jordan, Turkey, and Spain.

About the Consultant

Munir Shaikh oversees research and consulting activities at the Institute on Religion and Civic Values (IRCV), a non-advocacy organization with expertise in world religions, world history, civil society, pluralism, and related subjects. Munir has a master's degree in Islamic studies from the University of California, Los Angeles, and has more than fifteen years of experience in writing and editing texts pertaining to Islamic history and culture.

Photo Credits